Silent Squall

Also by Alfa:

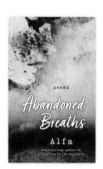

REVISED AND EXPANDED

poems

Silent Squall

Alfa

Bestselling author of
I Find You in the Darkness

Castle Point Books
New York

www.stmartins.com
www.castlepointbooks.com

The Castle Point Books trademark is owned by Castle Point
Publishing, LLC. Castle Point books are published and distributed
by St. Martin's Press.

Cover design by Katie Jennings Campbell
Interior design by Joanna Williams

ISBN 978-1-250-23359-2 (trade paperback)

Images used under license by Shutterstock.com

Our books may be purchased in bulk for promotional,
educational, or business use. Please contact your local
bookseller or the Macmillan Corporate and Premium Sales
Department at 1-800-221-7945, extension 5442, or by email
at MacmillanSpecialMarkets@macmillan.com.

Originally self-published by AlfaWorldwide
First Castle Point Edition: February 2019

10 9 8 7 6 5 4 3 2

This book contains descriptions of domestic abuse,
which may be difficult for some readers.
For more information on domestic abuse and
how to recognize its signs, contact the
National Domestic Violence Hotline by calling
1-800-799-7233 or at www.thehotline.org/.

This book is dedicated
to those who loved *Abandoned Breaths*
enough to let the words breathe,
and to everyone who fights the stigma
of heartache. You are not weak
because you feel.

You are the strongest souls I know.

Everyone becomes a poet when their
hearts are screaming.

Contents

Introduction

I decided to write this book after being asked so many times how my first book, *Abandoned Breaths*, began.

Silent Squall touches upon emotional and physical abuse. It deals with the horror of finding yourself in the middle of a life that is ruthlessly controlled by *the one* who professes to love you. Your mind and your body become bent—always at the beck and call of the *watchman.* Your self-worth is discarded because he strives hard to make sure you are void of it. You are broken down, sliced in slivers, and each day of this becomes your normalcy... *yet you know it is not normal.* You hide from friends behind smoke and mirrors, because no one can know the truth. They might think you deserved it. You've become weak, but this is his plan. *That way you cannot flee.*

One day you will determine that anything is better than not wanting to live anymore. *And somehow you gain the courage to fly.* You may do it silently in the middle of the night or you may require law enforcement or friends and family to guard your back... *but you fly.* You sever the legal ties, yet the struggle continues because the road to freedom is long and your abuser is vicious.

These poems and quotes are about a journey. An ongoing pilgrimage of finding the person I lost in the storm 30 years ago.

Many of these quotes and poems were first written in a journal I began while in therapy. It is my hope that if you are in any situation similar to this that you *tell someone*. I hope that this book gives you the courage to take flight and to begin living again.

We Have Work to Do

She is kind, in a no-nonsense way.

It feels strange speaking to a medical professional about the personal and broken parts *inside* me. I'm on the other end of the desk. *I'm used to talking one on one with my patients.* Yet here I am... sick. *I want you to write down the first thing that comes to your mind and we'll take it from there.* She wants me to use my love of words as therapy. She hands me a canary yellow notebook, a tool to help me release my emotions. She doesn't know I've already been doing this for over 30 years. She tells me to bring it with me each visit.

The following day, when she reads my first entry, she sighs. "We *have work to do.*"

I tried so hard, but I could never make this world love me.

There are moments in time

that your mind will never allow you to forget. A fragrance, a nostalgic scent that you identify *with one person* aids in mental recall. *Autumn is a trigger for me.* I smell the heaviness of the ombre leaves as they begin their great descent, and the memories cascade like raindrops from heaven. *A kiss on the bank of a swollen river whilst my toes sink into sticky mud that feels like chocolate frosting. Broad shoulders below me, bent knees, trembling like the strings of a guitar—asking if I will be his for a lifetime.* There was no exaggeration in his tone, and I wish I had known then that he meant every rehearsed syllable, while stroking my youthful soul with the words a naïve girl longs to hear. *Lifetime.* Because even after all these years, there are days that I still feel like I belong to him—*and he to me.* And I shake myself awake, and remind my lungs to breathe, because I'd rather die than be back there, in that lifetime, *willing myself to believe in another day.*

The thing is, I spent most of our years together trying to find a way out. And no one knew.

It was him or me, and I decided—I wanted to live.

Flight

Understand

I'm standing in a palatial courtroom that dates back before the Civil War. The smell of 160 years of furniture polish and cleaning solutions weighs heavily in my lungs, and I try in vain not to breathe in through my nose. Their odor has not disinfected the permanence of all souls who have stood here before me.

I feel them. I hear them warning me, telling me there is a deadly fight before me. At this point, I am just numb.

It's taken me sixteen years to get here, and can any battle compare to what has led me here? I've reached a point where nothing else matters except my sanity, and most days I cannot find any evidence of that either.

I hear the judge say my name, and I look up into eyes that are curious and searching— and a flicker of hope begins to burn within my chest.

Not like the time he held me against the wall with one arm for fifteen minutes, and I couldn't wear a bra for three weeks because my insides burned so badly. *Not that kind of burn.* But I feel an authentic, hopeful flame burning within me. Maybe, just maybe, she will be the one to understand.

Does He Hit You?

Blows without hands.

Each strike a verbal assault.
Intimidation with a stare.

Cleansing

I know my worth… now.

My therapy sessions are paying off. There was a time when I did not think I was worth two corroded pennies rubbed together.

My therapist claims this is normal.

But, if I had to pinpoint a time
in my life when I felt as worthless
and as meaningless as hot dog scum—

yes, it's real stuff—it would be the awakening
my *twenty-something-year-old-self*
had while scrubbing 30-year-old, once-white
bathroom tile grout with a nail file at 3 a.m.

While the babies and my husband slept, I
labored over the most ridiculous of tasks,
trying in vain to make
our helter-skelter lives pristine, Mayberryish
and fairytale like.

I thought that bleach, Pine Sol,
and elbow grease could wash the pain away,
send the misery gurgling down the drain.

In some twisted way, I hoped
the cleanliness I tried to impart
would wash the filth away from my soiled soul.
I felt dirty… and used. Spoiled goods.

I was dependent upon a man for my emotional and physical stability.

My lot in life was to please him, not rile him.

Please him: always my thoughts were of pleasing him.

Make him happy. Keep him calm.

The kids don't need to hear him angry. He will ignore them if he's mad at me. He likes the house clean.

Clean… makes him… tolerable.

The carpets require vacuum marks—just so. One direction. Unified. Back and forth.

The bathroom should be immaculate. Wash and shine shampoo bottles.

Fold the towels just right. Creases left and right.

The tile must glow. The grout is old…

my fingers are raw and peeling. Droplets of my blood are on the canvas. The bleach burns… but scour, I will.

I must prove to this man who thinks I'm nothing that I have worth.

(continued…)

I must justify my worthiness to myself.

So, as I sat there on that cold tile, inhaling bleach fumes, scrubbing

with bleeding fingers, *and hating myself all the while, knowing that my life was a delusional screwed-up mess*.

I had an awakening.

I did not want to feel worthless anymore.
I wanted it all to go away.

I wanted to start a new life. Begin again.

Blink and make it all go away.

Little did I know, it would take hundreds of these self-awakening cleaning sprees before I acquired the strength

to shake out my fearful feathers, and fly.

Looking Back

I look back on occasion.

It takes only seconds

to recall the parts of me

that I've had to leave behind. All the
dirty fragments

I've tried to bury will resurrect

and reassemble for a glimpse.

I look back because it forces me to remember
that I've battled as valiantly

as any love-starved fool

for the peace I now possess.
I can say this now…

"You'll look back one day.

You'll realize all the things you tossed and
turned over were not worth

getting into bed with, much less worrying
about."

Doing Without

I find ways to numb the pain.

I write.

I release.

And then I hide the notebooks under the blue shag carpet

in the broom closet.

I keep your world immaculate.

I try to please you when I know there is no way to please someone *who is displeased with life.*

I manage—*doing without,*

so your lifestyle does not change. The children you take credit for are so beautiful. I wish you knew

them.

I ask myself:

"How can I hate you, when you gave me something so beautiful?"

An Autumn Soul

One day the leaves begin to change,

along with the love you thought you were in.

You blink against your will, and feel your
heart begin to unravel…

shredding into pieces, as the person who you
deemed different begins to change along with
the season.

You mouth goodbye as he blends in

with hues of bad decisions,
jack-o-lantern masks,

and pumpkin-spiced kisses.

And you know how the leaves feel

as they fall, dying, onto the ground.

Pity

There are those

who mistake her sorrowful eyes for weak ones.

They connect pain with weakness, or with
one's inability

to handle its destruction.

They look away,

with pity riding

their judgmental spines. What they do not
understand is that her strength

grew from pain…

and that she had become her very own

superhero.

It is *those* people

who never stopped gawking long enough

to offer a helping hand. Because, sometimes,
people see what they want to see.

Grasping Heartache

Why do our souls hold on to fairytales,

and our hearts grasp heartache?

Two Percent

When you look at me,

What is it you see? *How do I stack up?*

You are much too observant not to categorize
me or to tally my mistakes. Have you analyzed
me from head to toe, *like my therapist does
weekly,* and made a discovery, a diagnosis?
What is it I suffer from? Is it too much, or are
my past aches lacking in your eyes? I have
shown you two percent—mere minutes—and you
think you know the 98 proof I have bled for
years. I've lain on white tile, swimming in
red, and prayed for anything but breath.
I've begged for food to feed mouths that were
not mine, and I have slept hungry an entire
marriage. I have had the dignity slapped
from my face, along with every hopeful dream
I possessed.

And there are days... I am back there.

Reliving every moment.

And that's only two percent of me.

Destruction

You left the wind

with your exit.

It nearly flattened me, but that's the thing
about weathered souls.

Storms with names like yours

unleash our inner strength. Our reserves are
layers deep, and we become experts

at learning to rebuild

after our foundations

are ripped away

by surfboarders,

stopping by on frothy waves.

We are survivors

of the human heart condition.

A New Season

Today I feel human.

It is the first time since you left that I have
woken up

and wanted to look outside.

I ache to see trees budding,

and the sage-infused grass blowing caches of
stored leaves.

A storm brews as cotton clouds turn to
nicotine smoke

on the east side.

It will not be long now, and the heavens will
open and water winter's neglect.

With spring comes a chest full of hope
and I walk outside

to absorb the mist rising off the pavement.

I breathe in the rain

that has come from nowhere,

just as I knew it would, and I love the way

the air tastes as it crawls its way around my
chest. Like magic, the gray skies roll back to
highlight a sun

so bright that dewy daffodils stand tall and
vie for attention.

And it occurs to me, that just like that, our
lives can change.

One minute foreboding storms, and then
mesmerized by glorious views we can see
forever.

It is all so necessary. Would we appreciate one
without the other?

The Dance

My screams climb high

and dance in my throat. A tango trying to
let go, aching to be heard.

I've never learned the art of letting go.

I've painted pretty pictures with the best of
intentions. Brush strokes meant to reveal
and release…

But they are counterfeit. Copies of the flesh

I long to shed.

The original hangs on a wall in my soul…

Cobwebbed and dust caked. Welcoming me
whenever I visit.

Visitors

Your cobwebbed heart with rusty iron gates

is euphoric to them.

They want to enter…

they want to *spend the night*

in your icy rooms

and peek in your ransacked closets.

They get prickles from the barren,

the forlorn, and the pain that hurting
hearts exhibit. These people are sightseers,
visitors…

but they never stay.

Caravans

How do you explain

the absence of a person to your soul?

I have the advantage here.

I'm writing about this after a significant
amount of time has passed.

My wounds aren't fresh… but they're still deep.

Time primes your heart.

The ache is still with you every day, but you'll
find it is more bearable on day 12,452 than on
day seven.

And it's simply because your heart

has become encased in a fortified covering
that is almost impenetrable.

The years of growth and neglect have made

it fine pickings for a paranormal ghost tour—
but I pity the caravan that comes gawking.

You see, there are people entranced
by anything

ghostly and dark.

Ransom

It was in the darkness

that I reached,

clutching memories that ran down

a prideful spine.

What could have been

the echo

of a banshee's last wail.

I did not willingly

let half of my soul

leave my body.

It was torn from me.

I still hear ransomed moans.

It calls to me for rescue,

yet clings to its abductor.

Examine Within

You are going to question yourself.

Beat yourself up with self-doubt, remorse, and regret.

After you stop blaming him you will start blaming yourself.

The interrogation turns inward
with a right hook you never saw coming.

You will place your heart
on the witness stand and you
will be thorough in your technique.
When someone walks away,
we always turn the mirror around.
We examine within.

We pick ourselves apart… piece by piece,
and we are unforgiving in our punishment.

If you did not love yourself before, or at
least like yourself a little… you are going
to shatter.

We have all been there. Immersed in pain.
The breath-catching kind
that renders you emotionally bereft.
Implosion.

It's times like this that you
must hold on to your self-worth.
Or at least try to.

It's hidden down a long slippery slope.

Hold tight to a measure of self-love.

Grasp it with all you have left.

Wrap yourself in the arms of your
outstretched soul.

Comfort yourself.

There's always the faintest of lines between
love and hate

when someone chooses to leave you.

But, don't hate.

Don't hate a person you once loved because
they've left you.

Nothing will impale your soul with such force

as replacing love with hate. Love yourself...

That kind of love will get you through

any kind of heartache.

That... and time.

Residue

How do I make you feel it?

Tunneling between my ribs, the ache
that molds

and reduces my curves to fragmented lines.

I want to scrape you from my insides.

Rid myself of your smell. It is a part of me,

seeping from my core. Tangled with the fright
and the angst I carry.

I harbor townhomes of our past.

A community built upon

a ground with no foundation. The ghastly,
incessant shaking at the mere thought

of seeing you again

is rendering me mosaic. I've spent half my life
in your vision,

married to your last name,

and I want none of it. No more.

But you keep on haunting. The memories will not leave. Everywhere I look, I see you.

I see the dirt you've left behind, and I find myself cleaning

up after you, even when you

are no longer here.

I peek behind doors.

I hear you breathing at night and I pat the bed to make sure you are really gone.

I do not talk above a whisper in case you can still hear me. You're not here,

but you're still everywhere.

Earthquake

My soul was an earthquake.

Always on edge in fear of you.

Orchestrated

I used to fear the air

coming in and out of my lungs,
because you were

a part of *every breath.*

Each inhalation was orchestrated
by your hand…

I feared I could not

do something *as simple*

as take in

and release air.

My Government

You tower over me.

Your shadow is my government.

You hurl words that my cowering self thinks
are deserved.

I play dumb because it makes you appear
intelligent.

Everything about me is hidden.

My beauty you once loved

is packed away between crisp eyelet sheets;
tucked in a balsam-wood hope chest

that you never let me open.

All my youth lies at the bottom of an
unused bed,

held prisoner with a cellmate of hope.

Strangle

You tried.

But your hands could never quiet her soul.

I Feel Everything

I feel everything.

I look around,

and I try to see the world the same way you do.

But…

I see noise.

I hear colors.

I feel everything.

My answers have no questions and my words have no rhyme. I'm empathetic to a fault, but my bones are numb. I scream from morning to night, but my vocal cords hum into silence.

I see noise.

I hear colors.

I feel everything.

Support

Eventually you will reach a point where you observe and take stock of the support system in the foundation of your life. You decide to remove the ornamental, and you pledge to give back to everyone who has uplifted you, loved you, *and stood by you.*

Heavy Times

Days spent in listless embodiment.

Praying for death but wanting so badly to choose to live.

Clinging to the molecules in the air as a reason to open swollen eyes.

Climbing imaginary cliffs and free-falling.

Feeling the wind blow tear-soaked hair, as the troubles lie heavily behind.

Ancestry

When you have had enough, your soul will rise
up with the strength of your ancestors,

each one holding luminous lanterns, lighting
the trail to ensure you escape

the darkness.

Missing Someone

You can miss someone whom your heart hates...

Did you know that?

It doesn't mean you want them back; quite the contrary, you do not at all...

but you're a newborn learning to live life again, and your breaths are for one and not two.

And it will seem labored and empty, breathing in the air they once occupied.

You'll find yourself blank-faced, head between your legs, inhaling. Feeling like you're missing something. You take in full, deep breaths that you've been holding, thinking everything in your life up to this point was all a dream.

You don't want the part back that you have cut out. You don't. You can miss the person whom you once upon a time thought was your fairytale.

You can miss the normalcy and the routine of a life that you worked so hard at—and all for naught.

Because, *Poof*. You're free. Finally, free.

And you're alone.

And you're breathing.

But the emotional ties are still harnessed tightly to yesterday, and you're trying to figure out how to survive tomorrow.

Safe Place

I am sitting cross-legged

in a closet that smells of one hundred years
of decay and stored memories. Faded peony
wallpaper covers plaster walls, and I can tell
you there are 241 blooms from top to bottom
and side to side. I have carved a seat amid the
storage. A place for me to sit and contemplate
survival. I count backwards from 100, and
when I get to 37, I breathe. When the world is
closing in, I close myself in here. I should be
frightened, even nauseated, by the
confinement. It is dank and exudes odors of
old cedar and the previous owners' clothes.
There are mice here, but I don't look down
when I hear them scurrying. I have found a
place where no one else wants to be. They don't
look for me here. I think about tomorrow and I
wonder how I will walk among the normal
people. I feel another wave hit me. Drumrolls
in my ears. I clutch my chest. It hurts to
inhale. I pray and cry and pray and cry. I am
24 years young, but I feel as old as the
flowers lining the walls. I pray and cry.
I pray… and cry.

Freedom

One day

your soul

will get sick

of crawling,

find its legs,

and walk

right out the door.

Still Here

What is it about love

and the way it breaks you, then pulses within
every jagged shard?

A Rambling Run

A lifetime spent

running through hedges of knockout roses
bejeweled with thorns. Dreaming of strolling
amid mountains decorated with

love-me-not daisies.

Find Yourself

Don't forget to let yourself grieve

the love you have lost.

Loss is loss, no matter if they were yanked out of your life or you shoved them out the door. If you try to refill the gap too quickly, you'll never understand why you allowed yourself to walk around empty for so long.

Find yourself before you find someone else.

Surprise

The beginnings of relationships

never look like the endings.

We are often amazed,

when severing ties,

at how much people change.

You will look at them

and see a stranger with no heart

and think to yourself

there is no way

this person once professed

to love me.

Awareness

How do you know

they aren't the one?

At the first sight of total disregard for
your hurt,

your gut will feel uneasy.

I'm reminding you to listen up.

Spirit Slayer

You don't have to lay hands on someone to
murder their spirit. All you have to do is
withhold the love you promised them.

Control

You coveted me.

A young mind in need of love.

Looking for that filler that my youth lacked.
You molded me.

A slave for your desires.

An accomplice in your misery. Bonnie to
your Clyde.

You tried to make me hate the world

the way you do.

But, I can never hate something that calls out
to me with promises of freedom.

Passed Down

I started writing as a five-year-old who was afraid to speak because of the nuns who would strike my fingers with smooth wooden rulers. Now I compose thoughts that my daughter can read one day when she cannot find her own voice. Maybe she will identify with some, and maybe not. But, she will know her mother had layers that she never peeled back, for fear that her soul would seem chilly when unclothed.

Interlopers

I wonder how many of our present
relationships are sabotaged by past
intruders.

The interlopers who came and went like the
seasons. Always basking for weeks and then
craving the change and newness that
momentarily make their bones feel. Each
leaving impaled dents, and those creases are
felt forever.

A heart never drives the same way after it
crashes. It handles differently. It changes
direction and takes an alternate route,
afraid to travel the same road

again.

Sucker Punch

I wouldn't be human if I didn't beat myself up
on occasion. The problem is, I can take a
sucker punch with nary a flinch because my
pain tolerance is carved into a state of Zen.

Shaken

I write down the hidden thoughts my war-torn
heart has held tight, always fearing the world
will not

love me. I offer my voice in ink, a legacy for
my daughter.

Our daughters.

Maybe they will see that I was friction
beneath soft skin.

That I held an earthquake between the molten
lava attempting to erupt in my soul... the
world and its restrictions securing my
ribcage.

Maybe they will see that I screamed the
loudest I could, and that some cries often
pulse in silence.

Maybe they will know I battled in the confines
of the rules and dark rooms in which I was
sequestered.

Maybe when they read my words, they will
find their own, and not carry earthquakes
of the past.

But if they do, maybe they will shudder
and rock,

coast to coast,

and know they are never alone...

and maybe they will shake with a voice that is
silent no more.

What They Want to See

The ones on the outside looking in—they ask
for advice.

My scars must be covered today, because
they tell me they want my life. They want to
know how to attract the right man and keep
him happy.

I want to tell them to do everything

I did not do.

Run…

Their fairytales include a nice house,
a new car, and two-point-five kids.

I tell them the right one will come along.

It's true. People always see what they want
to see.

Hidden Rooms

I ache in hidden rooms that have gone
unexplored for too many years.

Lay That Sword Down

Sweet girl of mine, lay that sword down.

You are exhausted, and I fear you will fall.

I see your soul screaming in those eyes that are so much like mine.

Tread easy.

Waging war on the past is the final acknowledgment to the Universe that we are regretful about our yesterdays.

Don't be so hard on yourself about past mistakes.

The truth is, we're going to leave the ones who never really left, and we'll stay with the ones we should have left.

And those decisions change the entire course of our lives.

Go gentle on that heart that I admire.

The battle is not about correcting the past.

It's about you loving you—in spite of the guilt you feel.

I know it is hard, but you have to live for today...

and let yesterday go.

Is This It?

I cannot breathe.

My face is pressed against clouds

and gingham cotton, but I'm not floating.

Hands are pressing down,

pushing me from slumber.

I grab onto wrists I know all too well,

and I am rewarded with a knee in the stomach.

I cannot fight this time.

I feel life leaving me.

I'm half asleep and I still don't know

if I'm dreaming or not.

I feel myself giving up

as I hear an angelic voice.

Air reaches my face

and I struggle to drink it in, reeling.

And I hear my eight-year-old ask,

"Daddy, what are you doing to Mommy?"

Being There

We can justify

our self-neglect

in many ways,

but I have realized

that I make up

for not being there

for myself,

by always being there

for others.

In the Air

Absentee

I was a cow, and if he wasn't getting milk from the cow any longer, he was not going to pay for the calves, *nor nurture them.*

To him, parenting ended and began with the mother. If the mother was not in his life, neither were the children.

Losing His Grip

I am a pathetic mother.

I did not deserve to bear his children.

I caused nothing but strife, and I was the worst wife he could have been shackled with.

I wrecked his world.

Hearing these things in a courtroom full of strangers does little for your inner warrior princess, even if you know they aren't true.

I was told he would do this.

Gaslight me. I expected no less.

I've heard the venom spewing from his mouth for years.

Let them hear it.

How could a man who never admitted to any wrongdoing during his lifetime do anything else but blame the person he was losing control over?

My therapist calls him a narcissist.

I prefer the obvious: evil.

Yes, I was wrecking his world.

His Silent Squall was escaping his grasp...

and the man was losing his grip on reality.

Have Mercy

Being isolated from family and friends

puts you at the mercy of a person who wants to control you and puppet your fears.

You will become what he wants you to believe you are.

He creates you—in a sense, never giving you the chance to develop into your true self.

And for a time, you will think your life is normal.

Because to the outside world it looks that way.

Scavenger Hunt

I lost so many parts of me while loving you.
The recovery has been a scavenger hunt.
Locating my heart has proven to be the
ultimate goal.

Self-Approval

You strive so hard

thinking you can somehow

prove your worth

and your validity.

Imagine if you wanted the same

approval from your own self.

Roommates

I will never understand how the human heart
is capable of holding such glorious love and
putrid hate in its confines at the same time.

Never Disrespect Yourself

How to raise sons who respect women:

Never give them the opportunity to see you disrespect yourself.

Everlasting

I have singed wings,

and the edges of my heart

are charred

and crisped by flames

of your dismissal.

Yet, even though I sift

through ashes of the past

as I maneuver through tomorrow...

my soul's fingerprint

will be everlasting.

Poker

You will never find the comfort

from the ones who play poker with pain.

They will see you as a competitor.

They will play their stacked hand

against yours at every turn.

Their goal is to make your hurt insignificant

by always bringing focus back to themselves.

Leave the table.

Your priceless heart

is worth too much to gamble away.

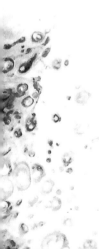

Mirror Mocking

The strength will come

with experiences.

One day you will be able to eat pizza again

without thinking of how much he
loved pepperoni.

Your heart won't capsize

every time the phone sings.

You won't spend hours looking at yourself in
the mirror, finding flaw after flaw.

Finding not one thing about yourself to love...

wondering if the scars you see mocking you

are what drove him away.

Classy

She is lovely because she has more class in
the layers of her soul than those who layer
their personalities for approval.

Experience

Promise me this:

When you find yourself in need of inspiration,

bypass the roses that will clamor endlessly
for attention.

And focus on the souls who have actually lived
among the thorns.

Bully

He fights to see me fail.

He has resorted to using his frame
against mine.

He learned early on that his wits were
smaller than mine, so he uses his mouth
and his hands, instead of his mind.

Broken Ones

Why do we hang on to the broken ones?

The broken words we never release.

The broken hearts that never increase.

Snatched

Completely

and without warning.

Ripped from my life

like a breath snatched from a soul.

And after all this time…

I plead with myself

to breathe in.

And I pray to the Universe

to give back

what it took away.

Tape Recorder

And here I am again,

back where you left me.

I press the worn buttons of my mind

and our last conversation

starts to play like clockwork.

I hear the even pitch

of words meant to soothe

but are gravel to my soul

and too carefully practiced.

They are saying everything

that is required to end your part in our story...

yet do nothing to ease the impact on my heart.

Not Less

I refuse to think I'm less…
than I *should* be.

Taillights and Tears

There is a grapefruit lodged

between my throat and my chest.

I put it there by telling myself

I deserved the pain.

The residue from swallowing every foul word

force-fed down my throat.

My excuse is I was hungry for love

and drunk on the idea of forever.

It seems grapefruits form in the aftermath

of taillights and tears.

Untouched

Sunshine peeks through eggplant drapes
alerting me of your tiptoed arrival.

I've been awake for hours—prepared to act like
I'm sleeping.

Your shift ended over seven hours ago,
and I smell you before you enter the room.

You've came home wearing the scent of a Friday
night well spent. I inhale the familiar breeze
of booze, mingled with an unfamiliar whiff of
jasmine perfume.

You lower your work clothes quietly, laboring
to stand upright. Years of practice has made
you an expert at shedding six pieces in a
little under 12 seconds.

I feel the bed shift, and I lie frozen,
feigning sleep.

Fake snoring is my superpower in times
like these.

I've perfected and can mimic the sounds of
deep sleeping. Within four minutes, your rasps
signal you are passed out, and I know I can
ease out slowly.

I must go check on the children
before they wake up
and wake you up.

Later, as I put cereal in bowls and juice
in cups,

I think to myself that I am grateful to the one
who served your ego and satisfied the hands
that left me untouched this morning.

Heartbreak Hotel

I am a collection

I am not overly proud of.

I absorb everything

that makes an imprint in my eyes.

So it should come as no surprise

that my heart has attached itself

to dark intentions,

along with the joyful ones.

Good and evil are always fighting

over the penthouse suite in my
Heartbreak Hotel.

And it is a toss-up,

who will be singing tonight.

Waltzing with Wolves

I have waltzed

and howled at the moon.

But, my heart will always remember

the slow dance

that ended much too soon.

On Sale

I allowed my feelings to become discounted,
barely yard-sale worth. I was giving my heart
away for pennies to those who wanted
something for nothing.

You Sleep

You sleep, I watch.

Your grandma's coverlet tucked around
broad shoulders.

Snug, barricaded, locked in on all sides.

Perfectly tucked over and under.

Your chest rises and falls in confinement.

I watch.

You sleep the same way you control our
marriage. Restricted.

Suffocating.

Bundled and rolled.

No room for escape.

Prison.

Wearing My Past

I may wear

my past

upon my skin…

but my future burns brightly within the

fire raging

in my soul.

Ribcage

Memories have a heartbeat and tap on my
ribcage with a force

that cannot be denied entry.

Fool

I have searched

beneath mossy rocks

and rumpled beds.

Fell for promises

bequeathed from bar stools,

and romanticized

whispers

from sultry hearts

that were oftentimes

dead men walking.

Gone

That person you fell in love with

doesn't exist anymore.

The mask fell

when they walked out the door.

I Shed You

I shed you.

Every season I watch pieces of you unfurl,

and fall away.

My hopes and dreams in mourning at my feet.

I close my eyes to grieve, and without warning
there you are.

Taking root,

and budding within me.

Click

One day you're going to feel your spine click back in place.

Your heart has been carrying a heaviness,

and its weight has curved your spirit and your expectations into a shadow of the virtuous being you are.

You'll feel the connection.

The latching.

It will be a shift that will jolt you from your tormented, bent knees into a towering presence with brand-new resolve.

It will happen…

I promise you, something will trigger it.

And when you feel that strength tingling and finger-walking through your beat-up body, do not let anyone or anything stop you from rising upright to your full potential.

No One Knows

You look at someone who seems to have it all together and you assume they're happy, content, thriving. From our observation they have no reason to be depressed because their life looks downright amazing.

But, I believe some people just wear masks well.

It's how they get through the day. They put their masks on as easily as brushing their teeth.

They have to. If they gave in, or focused on what they were feeling, they would render themselves immobile.

The sad thing is, you can deny something in your mind

and still feel it stirring in your soul.

You can get through experiences, days of funk, holidays if necessary, only to collapse when your soul finally screams I can't, and it's in those blackest of times when you start to question your existence. You wish something, anything, would make it all go away.

A part of you wants to give up. Give in. You wish the inky hands of death would just take you, X you out of this freak show and put an end to your anguish.

And you pray for it, silently, lest someone hear your mind on its knees.

You open tear-stained lashes and see that you're still here. Breathing.

Your heart is still beating, and as it rages out of your chest, it shows no sign of taking directives.

Helpless. You are. At this moment in time, you are. You tell yourself it will get better, and some days it does. But the mask: you wear that mask like you're on the catwalk.

Make no mistake, the dark times will find you again…seeking you out like a lover who knows every muscle that needs rubbing.

Fondling every curve, despair will thread names of self-loathing and disrespect between each and every rib. You will down talk yourself until you will justify what the world tries to shove down your throat.

(continued…)

You'll reach for that mask again because it
helps hide the scars from beating yourself up.
You'll go shopping, and you'll buy a matching
cape that complements the mask because you
are a superhero.

But you'll pray for death again… and no one,
not even your closest friends, will know.

Deep

I hurt with a pain that is so much deeper
than physical.

Soar

Nothing surprises me within the realm of human nature and how a soul evolves when rocked by pain.

I'm not young anymore.

I'm older than most of my friends.

My social circle includes many doctors, writers, and artists, most much younger than me.

My heart aches as I listen to and read their passion-laced prose.

I know what they're going through.

I don't say those words lightly.

I know the struggle.

So, I will tell you what I tell them,

and I learned this the hard way:

It hurts growing wings.

But it's necessary, because you need them to fly when your soul decides to soar.

Your Universe

I live in your cosmos.
Strapped to shooting stars.

Change

I believe in change

because I have watched

it happen in my own heart.

It is an execution,

not an overnighter.

The tough part

is enduring the process.

You can't go through pain

and not change in some way.

Well-Meaning Lies

They will tell you that you have so much to live for.

That with time it gets better.

That he didn't deserve you anyway.

That it was all for the best.

That you will meet someone new.

That real love can never be broken.

They are comforting you. It's what they do.

They love you.

But it's all well-meaning lies.

No one can tell you why things happen in our pasts, nor the future feelings of our heart and soul.

We all feel differently, absorb pain with different intensity, and everyone rebounds differently.

The only part that has a smidgen of truth is time.

With time, your body will endure the pain

until it is a dull thud.

It's always there, but you can carry it.

Surviving Today

I used to worry about tomorrow, but that was before I survived today.

Now it is one breath at a time.

Never the Right Thing

How many times

did my heart lead me back,

to try again

to do the right thing?

I've found out a heart can lie.

Mine did...

because it was never the right thing.

One Last Try

I stand before you,

after all these years,

back-and-forth pleas,

bartered emotions,

whispers through tears.

A part of me wants to run,

and never ask why…

but my heart has led me here

for one last try.

Every Page

A heart unscathed has surely never lived.

Remember that when you're beating yourself up

over past mistakes.

You will find yourself in a place of discontent

years after he has come and gone.

You will replay the past in your mind

like you are re-reading a favorite book.

You know every word upon every worn page.

You know how it ends.

But you can't stop your heart from
remembering,

over and over again.

Savior

Love kills me.

But, will it ever save me?

Landing

Battling for Freedom

This is the 11th time

I appear in her courtroom in nine months.
She doesn't look amused. I'm happy she turns
that displeased *but perfectly enhanced upper
lip* in his direction, and not mine. She tells
him to quit looking my way—she does not
grant permission to do so. *"Eyes forward,
Mr. Hi-faaaa-lutin"* she orders. *"This court
will enforce the emergency protection order."*
I swear the walls breathe, sighing in
exhalation of gratitude and relief when she
pronounces these words. And my quivering
bones, which have been reduced to noodles,
plate themselves for a probable feast. He likes
to pick the meat off my bones during these
sessions. Later, I tell my legal team that if
he had fought for me during our marriage like
he battles now, we could have taken on the
world as one, and the Universe would have been
our own pasta palooza.

I am Her

I am softness behind steel. Tears beneath
focused vision.

A worn heart behind the glaring smile.

I am her.

I am the woman who is viewed

as desirable, or sometimes detestable, solely
based on my looks.

I am her.

Your mother. Your sister. Your daughter.

I am flowers and weeds, and my soul

is a landscape carved by ruthless gardeners.

I am her.

I am the woman you work alongside every day.

The one you sat next to on the bus.

The one you admired in the stairwell.

I am the one you kissed goodbye this morning.

The one who birthed your children.

I birthed you.

I am a woman.

I am her.

Initial Sparks

I always questioned why he wanted me, if the reasons he gave for leaving were the initial sparks that drew

him to me in the first place.

Nightmare Memories

Not all fairytales end with light and
happiness. Some are dark and foreboding and
stay that way. Your stomach aches from gorging
on apples, and the tale is filled with so much
gut-wrenching pain that it would never be a
good bedtime story. You think *My God, this must
be a dream, or maybe I'm starring in a horror
flick,* but the fog rolls back, you pinch
yourself, and you barely scream.

By his own hand,

I ate crow.

And I convinced myself it tasted just
like chicken.

Ruler

I don't think we mean to do it, but we always
measure a current love interest by the one

who rocked us to our core.

Entranced

Like a sunrise,

he always tried to return, after he saw her glow

illuminating

other shores.

Heart Caretaking

Hearts are a lot like flowers.

With every season they lose blooms,
their roots dig deeper,

and they may look a little worn,
but don't blink:

with a little caretaking,

they will flourish and rise again,

twice as spectacular.

Tied

In an instant,

a memory or a flashback will summon a wave of
rage that will teeter me for a millisecond.
I've become an expert at harnessing emotions,
so I have to check myself often, but I can't
prevent the onset, the charge that zaps my
heart on occasion.

You see, even though I'm past my past, I'm still
tethered to it. I still carry doubt by the
bucket load. I empty the weight when it starts
to spill and sloshes around my overworked
heart. But it inevitably replenishes, and my
chest becomes a keepsake of all that was, and
never will be.

I'm strong, but that is a heavy burden to bear.

Let it Flow

There are times like tonight

when the ink in my soul

is flowing boldly,

but dries before it hits the page.

My thoughts are expressive hues

and quilt the forest I purposely cower in,

but my follow-through is tainted

by past intruders,

and I tremble, hesitant.

Splaying the soul is not for all

—no matter if you feel led.

If I open the gate, what remains?

I Know How it Feels When the Madness Ensues

When it appears out of nowhere and whispers, "Boo." Your chest starts to fold upon itself as the rusty knife blade carves letters of fear across your sternum. Your eyes start to burn from the pressure of holding the reservoir capped, and as you feel the searing tears begin to form, you realize there is no tissue in sight. A bouquet of balloons has lodged inside the back of your throat and they are celebrating your discomfort. Your brave self is focusing, trying to command your mind and practice that languid meditation everyone harps about. And all the while your inner self is pleading with the monster that is approaching: *"Please don't let me lose it. Not here. Not again."*

I know how it feels when the madness ensues.

Heavy Sky

She has moments when she looks up

and is taken aback by the heavy sky

as it meets blowing trees with
outstretched limbs.

She tries to decipher a defining line,

the place where they connect

and lock in so flawlessly,

and she feels as though she belongs
somewhere in the middle of their natural
and accepting love.

And her spirit screams to leap,

to discard the darkness

that is encased in the unforgiving earth
it wrestles in.

Hindsight

Looking back,

I wish someone had told me I was not alone,

during all the times

my mind told me I was.

Repeat Over and Over

I woke up to heaviness in my chest this
morning. I could feel the imprint of
your footsteps.

Heavy. Foreboding. Intentional.

You always had that way about you. Leaving
your mark wherever you went.

You've been sleepwalking through my
soul again.

How many mornings will I feel the loss of you?
Groundhog Day, over and over.

Get up, repeat. Do over.

You left doors open and pieces of yourself
scattered all over.

My insides scream from the wreckage.
Loss in the disarray.

You've been sleepwalking through my
soul again.

And I wish for once… you would wake up.

Off the Beaten Path

Where do I begin?

I lost myself somewhere along the way.

Leaving light for dark.

Weeds in my hair and soot in my throat.

Chasing after butterflies disguised
as passions,

Arrogance unfurling their wings.

Off the beaten path.

Spending time in cocoons of the past.

Nowhere I needed to be.

I should have followed the ravens
for guidance.

They don't wear masks.

They dress their hunger in their eyes.

They are dependable.

You know they will still want your flesh,

even as you die,

piece by rotten piece.

They Gave You an Answer

You're going to tell me

that you deserve an answer

before you can move on.

And I'm going to sound brutal

and detached from reality

when I say that the minute

they exited your life

without a backward glance,

they gave you every answer

to every question

that is bottled up in your heart.

Immersion

I have dived too deep. Again, and again,

losing myself beneath the depths I swam
for you.

Immersion.

My soul breaststroking, racing against
the buzzer.

Drowning, rather than testing waters.

You Meet and You Click

Somewhere between weeks of texts, and drinks chased by the newness of it all, you think you're already in love. It's crisp and new. It's fresh and aromatic. The Universe has opened its star-filled chest and bestowed upon you a beacon of charismatic light that is proving irresistible. A galactic warrior princess with a heart shaped in the template of your own is fighting through the barricades around you,

and you are falling hard. She is aesthetically lovely, articulate, accomplished, and passionate.

She is positive about life, and it's so incredibly contagious, you're seeing a pulse where you once saw death. You love how responsive she is to your banter. She is a goal-setter, with limbs full of creativity, and a heart exploding with dreams.

You love the way she giggles when you create new pet names for her, and the way she smiles impulsively when she catches you looking at her unaware. You find yourself aching—No... seeking her company.

...And the air bends when she leaves the room.

You weigh her sparkling attributes, comparing them to exes of your past, and she shines so bright that you are blinded to anything but the good and effervescent. She's everything you've been looking for, and you are a breath away from crying out to the fathomless skies—and thanking them for finding her and sending her your way.

It's just been a few weeks—but she is perfect. You know it's fast and it's just the beginning,

but I must ask, "Can you really love her?"

She's artistic, and she has drawn you a map... planting a big red X across the destination to the treasure trove: her heart. If you took notes, you know why her relationships failed in the past, and you must know she's been chewed up and spit out more times than an infant's first foods.

How observant are you?

She's left you clues. She is leaving you manna, sumptuous morsels for you to choose from. If you partake, they will guide you along your journey. Checkpoints she needs to evaluate. She will watch your approach. She will take note of how you handle the scenery along your way.

(continued...)

She will see if you can really love her.

You see, it's easy to love someone who represents everything you've checked off your list. She looks like Christmas morning right now, but are you going to feel the same way when you unwrap the pretty packaging and see that her heart is as deep and dark as the blackest Halloween?

When the shine wears off, because it will, are you going to love the dull, everyday, muted version of the warrior princess you imagine her to be?

Because while she is all those things you've checked off in your mind…

She is so much more.

She is deeper than any wishing well, and you are only in love with one percent of her: the parts she has begrudgingly revealed.

You haven't been by her side for the years it took to create the person you now profess to admire. You haven't touched the surface of the history contained within her fortified soul.

You are in love with the layer she has let you see.

If you find after a few months that your admiration wanes, and that you could not handle how she dared to change, (which is another way of saying you never really knew her to begin with), you will start to withdraw and view her differently: she is no longer perfect and you are left wondering what happened. And you will inevitably move on.

And she knew you would. She has prepared for this. Because you could not really love her.

It's a cycle. People like the newness.

She's encountered your type before. They cast their hopes and dreams, and their ideal fantasy, onto the spine of another individual. They feed them and create an imaginary monster. It's easy. They have no past with them: they are a blank slate.

And they make the first few weeks so idyllic that it takes on the same feeling as a theme park. Exhilaration. The ultimate high.

But she's looking for THE ONE.

The one who does not run when the façade starts to fall. The one who embraces the mess along with the pristine. The one who resembles grains of sand, and no, she doesn't mind counting every one of them. The one who says, I love you, and she can feel it tingling to her toes. He doesn't run, because he isn't going anywhere without her once he finds her.

He's like the ocean, rolling up on her shore, washing all her doubts away. He looks at her like Christmas morning, and he plays poker with her ghosts under a full moon on Halloween.

And he will love her.

Renaissance

A renaissance is taking

place within my healing ribcage.

Vintage stitches are fusing.

Spirits of old are dancing,

waltzing past corners

of self-doubt and despair.

Encouraging steps of self-growth
and self-love.

It's giving birth to a new soul

that is not fearful of change

but welcomes the homecoming.

I Am

I am trembles

on rested skin,

laid bare on Sunday morning.

I am the thoughts

you try to decipher at 2 am.

Windblown tresses,

picnics,

and paper cups,

stained with red wine.

I am not what I appear,

but everything your heart fears.

The Rose Knows

There are those who like a freshly
budded rose.

They are drawn to how it stands out among
the dozen, how the petals are fastened and
closed tight,

protecting its center.

But once it starts to unfurl, and its fragrance
fills the air, and its brilliant color fades to
a muted shade, their interest wanes.

The thorns that make their stems resilient
are viewed as obstacles that keep the tender
at arm's length. But the rose knows.

The rose knows the one meant for her will
brave the thorns with bloodied palms if need
be, to hold her with arms that hold without
withholding.

To love is brave. He will be a warrior.

Integrate

Always remember that your presence
in someone's life is worth pursuing.
You don't need to attach yourself
to people who view your precious heart
as an option.
If they are not making an effort
to integrate you into their life,
then you are wasting valuable time
that you can never get back.

Find the One Percent

When things are bad,

what hurts the worst—

Your body, your mind, or your heart?

And when you begin

to feel your soul collapse,

willing the pain to end,

you need to find that one percent

crouching beneath

all of the despair.

It is hidden,

but I promise you

it's only dormant.

Find it.

Listen to it

when it begs you

to hold on.

Irreplaceable

I'm not easily replaceable, you know. The things that made you run are the same things that attracted you to me in the first place. Even now I feel you turning around, unable to break free.

He Wanted Me to Explain It

To tell him why I wore distance affixed to my soul like a badge of honor. And I wanted to tell him. I really did. But I didn't know where to begin. How do you find the origin? For as long as I can remember, I've felt that people are bad. That they were put on Earth to judge me. Nitpick. Find my flaws and highlight them. I feared strangers as a child, but if I'm honest, I feared people in general. With people come hidden agendas, and intentions, and I was always taught to be on guard. Not trusting people was ingrained into my core, and I've lived wielding a sword for a lifetime now.

I knew something wasn't right when I was 11.

I didn't want to go outside and play with other kids. Just the thought of it would render me sick with chest pains.

I am the Warrior of Avoidance.

I wouldn't answer the telephone when it rang. The shrill of the incessant clanging caused a knifing ache beneath my ribs, and I would put my hands over my ears and bend low to the floor until someone else answered it.

I knew the voice on the other end of that
machine was going to request something of me,
my interaction, and if I hadn't had the time to
properly prepare myself (emotionally) to
accept two minutes of dialogue, I could not
pick up the phone.

Surprises were not good. A knock on the door?
No. It went unanswered.

Every interaction or meeting had to be
planned. I had to self-talk and force myself to
act normal.

There… I said it. I never felt normal.

Truth be told, I didn't even want to hear
another person breathe in the air around me.
Any social contact made my heart race into
places a child should never venture. I could
not breathe. I didn't understand why. I found
myself hating people yet yearning for
attention at the same time.

This would always be my Achilles' heel.

Run. Chase. Avoid.

Talking to another soul has always ripped
mine in half,

(continued...)

and I still find myself speaking as rarely as
I can. I can do it. I can do it well. But I don't
like it. I want to. I hate to.

People mistake this for being shy, stuck-up, or
"backward," as I've been called so many times.
But it is so much more. Yes, I've managed over
time. I have good days now. I sought therapy. I
married. I parented. I have college degrees
and a successful career behind me.

I learned to hide it from the world. I endured
it. I forced my smile upon the Universe and
dove into experiences that made me nauseated
and throw up when I left. There were seasons
in my life when I delved into the temptations
of this screwed-up planet to bolster my
confidence. I'm not proud of those times—but I
will justify them to my last breath.

I get through. I persevere. It's easier now.
But, it's still here, living within me...

I was, and I am, an introvert. And I will
always feel like a solo being in a world of
multiples.

So, when he asked me to explain it. I did.

But I could not make him feel it.

And he left, because some people cannot grasp
the fact that people like me exist.

Hollow

I wish I could take back every ounce of my heart
that I gave away.

Does that make me selfish or just regretful?

All I know is that I'm left

with an empty, hollow space. Dark and dismal,

the spooky one on the block.

And even the vagrants

are afraid to take a peek inside.

Try Again

I'm tempted by the newness

to begin again.

I feel my jaw soften, and my resolve

hardens.

Let's try this again.

Rarity

He wanted you because you were rare
in his world.

I'm the Person
You Talk to Every Day

I'm the person you talk to every day

and you have no idea.

You have no knowledge of the strength it is
taking me to stand

and look you in the eye and speak.

You don't know that people like me

are silently screaming inside, and that those
screams haunt and wail 24 hours a day.

Heat of the Moment

We say things in the heat of the moment.

I think we've all done it. We are human, after all. We're not proud of it, and we can justify it to ourselves if our feelings somehow change.

But let someone else hurt us, or take back their words that they have promised, and we are ready to throw them into the middle of a bonfire.

It's devastating to think that at one time someone felt an emotion deeply enough to look you in the eyes and promise you forever… and then reneged.

Knee Jerker

There will come a time when you ache with a
loneliness that breaks you at your knees. And
you will realize that my presence in your life
was worth pursuing.

Normalcy

Red balloons, Tater Tots, and cupcakes for each new year. A celebration for one of the reasons my heart beats. I try to make this house feel like a home. I layer my dull luster and apply an outward shine. I smile for the icing-caked children as I serve, and count, and sing.

Compartmentalized. There is no mention that he is absent. It's become normalcy. Soap operas have nothing on me.

Out of Breath

I don't know

what it means

when people tell me to rest.

How do you stop a mind

from running through every past memory,
until the heart

is out of breath?

Inner Fire

There's a fire within me

that most will never see.

It has kept me warm during frigid times, when
my heart was frozen and refused to pulse.

When I could not leave my bed

for fear of the coldness in this world, the
flames nipped and enticed my soul,

thawing just enough of my arctic self-worth to
encourage me to try again, and again.

Ghosts

Some eyes are blank, and you know their
ghosts are sleeping, but then I see others…
and it looks like a paranormal convention.

Lettuce

I sit here in my universe, alone with thoughts of us and how we once were, and I ask myself if it is you I miss, *or if it was being a part of us.* A unit. Not having someone to rely on, to be your rock in times of trouble, is a terrifying reality. Not having someone who sees things through the same rose-colored glasses that you put on in the morning can be lonesome. You can't change people, you know? You can't add attributes they do not possess, either.

Yet we do it.

That's how we get into relationships that are doomed to fail. We think they will change.

You think you will be able to carve them—*give them tree trunk feet.* But the base is the same.

The foundation is the same.

Look at this person in the raw. That's what you got. You can dress a salad, but underneath it's still lettuce.

Dandelion Wish

She has a heart filled with hope,

and prays for the wind

to carry her dandelion wishes in search of
a fertile soul.

Yesterday

It's all the same, you know:

Silence. Rain drops.

Unmade beds. Cobwebbed hearts.
Unsent letters.

Yesterday. Today.

Tomorrow.

Desserts

Memories present themselves like decadent desserts. You promise yourself one bite, and then you realize your heart has become much too full, and you are left with crumbs of what used to be.

Hoarder

We carry the burden of yesterday.

We do. *Or at least some of us do.* How many times have you thought about emptying your heart and soul, *and putting them down?* Our memories are in our eyes and weigh heavy with every fragmented step. They are in our arms that endlessly reach, trying to grasp tomorrow. We drop pieces of the past and fill the crevices with momentary pleasure, trying to replace what we have lost. Memories— encasing you like your favorite jacket on a late December day. Keeping you warm and fuzzy and protecting you from the cold. It's a struggle, a pendulum swinging back and forth. We cling to the rock-hard surface, the sustainable dependability of our memories— gaining momentum, and for brief moments we feel enlightened and indestructible. They are our superpower. Hidden, yet seen. Absent, yet felt. They are our never-ending story. We know what was, what could have been, and what we hope to *feel* again. Our memory reel rolls endlessly. We can conjure up any episode to fit the mood. And for some reason we cannot let them go. *But oh, if we could only put them down.* Maybe we reminisce because we want our pasts back again, or maybe it's that we want something that resembles our former lives? A substitution. A repeat. Whatever the reason, we are hoarders, not of things, but of thoughts that bring us comfort and personal justification. We strive for validity because we know we were once capable of sewing our heartstrings in impenetrable stitches, inside the chest of another soul.

Memories. *I tell myself to put them down*, and all I do is raise them to eye level and see where I used to be.

Quake

You will feel a trembling in your soul

and out of instinct you will pray to silence it.

But do this for me. Do this for you.

Quake, sweet woman, quake.

They Come Back

I don't believe they go away and come back
because they finally decide that they love you.

Not all the time, anyway.

I think they come back because they use the
depths of your true love

as a bathtub.

They jump in and out every time they want to
feel clean and refreshed.

They come back because they know you
love them.

Conformed

I meet his stare and I see his appreciation.

I see it all in the way he looks me up and down, weighing the years. Balancing the wear and tear against the maintenance performed. I clean up pretty good. War paint covers a multitude of sins. He tells me I'm lovely, and I'm not sure why this bothers me as much as it does. Knowing that he sees the same slicked-up version of myself that I saw in the mirror earlier, I'm not surprised.

I conformed to please. I squeezed.

Squinted. Succumbed.

Poured the mold so many expect and masked my exterior pretty for the world this night. All he sees is the canvas, but not the brushstrokes.

He does not know the melding of the colors, or the carefully crafted application of texture that went into the statue that stands here before him.

They say it's time, and that I should begin to date again. I'm trying.

I feel my legs shake, but not for want of him. He does look handsome, and appears to have tried to impress, just my type, but no, my legs shake because I'm forcing them to walk toward another one.

Someone who is only interested in comeliness and outward beauty, artificial intelligence, and arm candy.

You see, I've sewn my hopes and dreams, my passions, and my longings inside my soul. I've meticulously fashioned them in Braille, and you must be blind to the Hollywood headlights of this world to read me. The one meant for me must travel through my universe with inquiring and curious hands and unearth the manifest I carry within.

He will understand that the depth of a woman is inside her body. He will want to fall in love with his eyes closed. He won't care about the book cover because the story I've scribed inside my veins will enamor his heart.

I am a novel, and I need to be read

repeatedly.

Responsibility

You blame yourself.

When will you let him take responsibility for the pain he inflicted?

Finding
Me

Self-Motivation

When you do not have anyone in your life to motivate you, you will have to inspire yourself to keep on keeping on.

I know, I know… where do you find the will?

The strength that is needed to rise up and go through motions that feel so foreign and fake?

Sometimes all it takes is remembering where you used to be and where you never want to return to.

Pitchfork

When you have lost everything, and you hold
on to fists full of dust, you will scoop the
sins you have hidden from your heart. You will
pull the past out and poke it with a pitchfork,
thinking that since you have lost all joy from
your life, you are deserving of the hell that
is caused by replaying what you have tried
to forget.

Authentic Self

How many times did you let them see your
authentic self?

Not the slicked-up, holding-it-all-together
package, but the seams-bursting, emotion-
spilling kind of unearthing that left your
heart and your knees raw?

How many times did you bare yourself
this way?

You don't want someone who will stay because
you conform perfectly to this world. You
deserve the one who will take a knee, offer
a hand, and lift your spirit off the floor.
You will see the truth in others by living
true to yourself.

Unstoppable

And I've noticed that since you've been gone,

I am unearthing this creature that scares the hell out of me.

She is fierce,

and unstoppable in her quest to become the best version of herself that she can be.

And I wonder if it took your leaving before she felt safe enough to show her scars to the world.

Ongoing Love

Love has found me many times during this lifetime.

Hopelessly besotted and rocked to the core…

But the love I have for my children is the only love that split my soul with each birth, and still miraculously multiplies with each year I am their mother.

Never Satisfied

They go from picking your heart out of
a crowd,

to picking it apart,

highlighting

        every

           flaw.

She Feels the Walls Move

She feels the walls move.

So close her fingers graze each side.

In times like this, she runs.

She knows the weight will knock her to
the floor.

So, she runs for solitude, lest someone see her
strength ebb and her smile crumble.

She knows she needs help, and she wants it.

She scrolls through her phone, panicked.

Who would understand the grip that threatens
to strangle her words?

So, she scrolls down.

And name after name goes by.

No one would understand.

She feels the walls move, and she runs.

Lucid Ribbons

Hearts weep.

I hear mine wailing

in the ink of the night.

The sobbing wrenches

my ribcage,

and I force my body

to go rigid.

To brace myself

for the onslaught

of memories

and lucid ribbons

that will inevitably

accompany such despair.

Oh, How the Heart Weeps

I shudder as each somber wave massages my insides, *much like his hands once did.* The heart is a lover, through and through. Every bit of its hurt is released throughout my body, every capillary is filled by its pain. Brilliant in questions, I sigh as I feel it coursing through my bloodstream. *Oh, how the heart weeps.* And it is a cry I cannot find a way to comfort.

Choo Choo

Our love was like a train

traveling too fast

at midnight

with a sleep-deprived driver.

Unveiled

I'm left with transparency.

My mystery is gone

and has been replaced

with acceptance.

No more secrecy

or hiding behind

the anonymity

of love.

What You Left

It's true. You may have taken everything with you when you left. I find emptiness in my deepest crevices and voids in the air my hands flail through.

But you did leave one thing, and it lives and breathes with a power that controls my heart's rhythm.

And that is memories.

And I don't know why you couldn't fit them in your suitcase with everything else.

Leaving You

The thought of leaving you in the past

renders me numb.

How can I abandon you

the same way you did me?

Nightly Funeral

I have funerals *in my mind* every night.

Candles illuminate the black lace I've dressed in so as *not to feel out of place in my bed.* The flowers I have filling the room are always too fragrant—*depressingly happy.* I've searched the world over and I have never found a sad flower. I see familiar faces marred with sadness, lined with regret. One by one they pass by in my mental screen. I reach out. I can be the warrior here. The one who comforts loved ones. I give a theatrical eulogy and I bless the crowd with all of your attributes. I save the not-so-pretty parts because they only need to know the best of you. *But I never let myself get to the actual burial.* I'm not ready to watch the dirt fall into the pit, *even though I could envision it a landslide of needed goodbyes.*

Force-Feeding

Have you ever tasted your tears

as they mixed with the food

your friends tried to force

down your throat?

Needed to Know

You and I

were always

on a "need to know" basis…

because

I

always

needed

to know.

Real Talk

Are you one of those

who speak from the gut

and do not recite the lies

your heart will try

to convince you of?

Thief

When they can run

from the responsibility

that coincides with love,

never let them take

your heart with them.

Hors D'oeuvres

Tell me about the pieces you've lost. The ones you freely gave away as hors d'oeuvres amid candlelight dinners for two. Every night you sat broken at your table, staring at overcooked food that had been reheated one too many times. How many days did you waste offering comfort to him, only to have him find it somewhere else?

The Gallery

Don't paint yourself abstract

for the gallery

if the colors

of your soul

are simple and defined.

Choices

When he gave me

no choice

but to walk...

I ran.

Conquest

All he did was breathe life into my soul.

I was a conquest. An easy one,

and you don't know how badly it hurts

to know

I was used

and tried

for a time.

Then thrown back.

Lesson Learned

He was a bruise, not a tattoo.

Endurance

I am unbelieving in quick fixes.

Replacing someone too soon is a bandage that slides off with the first wash. Give the wounds time to heal, and when they are the faintest of scars, let them be a firm reminder of what you have endured. Don't run hell-bent into another relationship.

Walk with that beautiful head held high. You know what to expect now. You've faced tragedy and now have another chance at happiness. Smile and embrace it. No matter what happens, experience has taught you that you can get through anything.

Mercury Glass

Every time our hearts touch, we become mercury glass:

Opaque in our intention.

Brilliant in our desire.

The love is there, trial after trial, yet gets lost under grocery bags and medical bills, and the home we anxiously try to fill with things that scream "I'm here."

But when I pull the sheet back at night and climb in close, touching my heart next to yours,

we shine like mercury glass.

Forests of Forever

Months have passed since I have seen your face. Yet, I still wear your memory from head to toe like a weeping willow tree clings to her foliage for comfort.

I sob within until my exterior blends in with forests of forever—*the place where souls get lost* and are never seen again.

Ending

If I tell you the ending,

will it make the beginning

any less valuable?

Will it make the present

any less painful?

Let's play it out.

It's the only way to ensure

the entire story is written.

Then…

you can write

your ending.

Thunder

Let me tell you about her.

Her love is like thunder.

You'll feel her soul

enter your bones

long before the

lightning strikes

your heart.

Therapy Works

I planted myself within her patient hands

and she helped me sift through the memories.

I'm left with the inquisition of a heart

that is *much too experienced at calling me
to the witness stand*

to answer questions that always lead
to the inevitable:

"If he loved me, how could he hurt me?"

And while I know I will never have the answer
to that question,

I do know that *it was not my fault.*

I will forever be grateful to her for helping
me *feel* this.

Acknowledgments

To Kevin, my children, and my mom, who have had to endure my quirks and my hermit status. Thank you for loving me, and for learning to love a writer. *I love you all.*

To Jesus Christ. You are the reason in every season of my life. Thank you for taking me on the pathway that has led me to today.

A big thank you to everyone who loved *Abandoned Breaths*! This is for you!

About the Poet

Alfa would paint the world in hues of turquoise if she could. Unapologetic about her realistic take on heartache, she writes to let her readers know they are not alone in their pain. Her four children and three granddaughters, the stars of her life, were the catalysts that pushed her to force her words and her smile on the world after a lifetime of depression and anxiety. She wanted to leave something behind for them, a legacy, proof of existence, and proof that pain can be transformed into beautiful inspiration. Alfa lives in Louisville, Kentucky. You can find her on Instagram @alfa.poet and on Facebook: @alfawrites